At the Circus

Devised by
Peter Usborne

Illustrated by
Derek Collard
and Pace Studios

Macdonald Educational

Look at the people and the animals at the circus.   Look for
the dogs, the bears, the monkey and the tiger.   What are they
all doing?   What could happen to all of them?   Will the
elephant stay on the ball?   What will happen to the clown?

Will the tiger land on the stool? What will happen to the
bears? Is the monkey safe? Will the little girl finish her
ice cream? Think of all the things that could happen.
Now turn over and see.

Look what has happened.   Look back at the first picture.
Find all the things which have changed.   What has happened to
the elephant on the ball?   What has happened to the clown?
Where are the bears?

3

Did the tiger land on the stool? Is the ringmaster frightened?
Where is his hoop? What has happened to the green stool?
Where is the girl's ice cream? What do you think
could happen now?

1
2
3
4

How many horses are there? Count the riders and the clowns.
How many riders are men? How many are women? How many
people are wearing blue? How many are wearing red? How
many clowns are upside down?

How many tigers can you see?   How many lions and leopards?
How many animals are lying down?   How many are standing on
their hind legs?   How many are crossing the boxes in the middle?
Count the red things, the striped things and the spotted things.

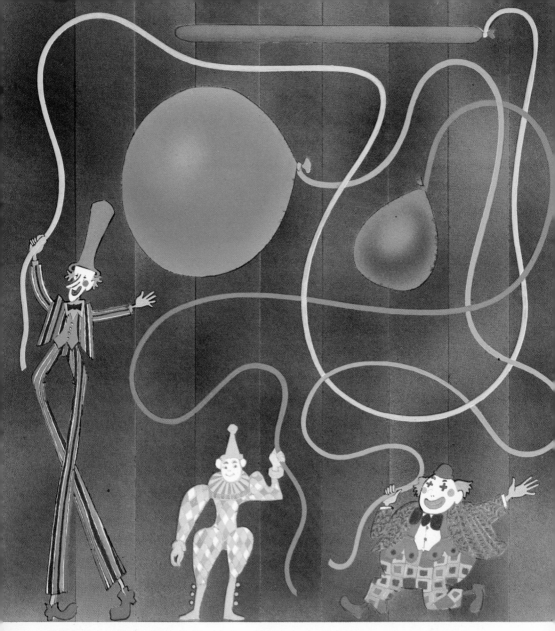

Which is the tallest clown? Which is the fattest? Which clown has the largest balloon? Which one has the longest balloon? Trace along the strings to find out.

7

Look at the clowns round the edge of the picture. What is
each one doing? Find a coloured space in the middle where
each one would fit.

8

Look at all the people and the animals.   What are they all
doing?   What are the horses and the elephants doing?   Can
you see a man on a tightrope?   Do you think he will fall?

Look for all the acrobats.   Look for the ringmaster.   Find
the lady selling sweets.   Can you see someone with an
ice cream?

Look at the tent being put up.   Now look at the shapes at
the bottom of the page.   Find shapes like these in the picture.

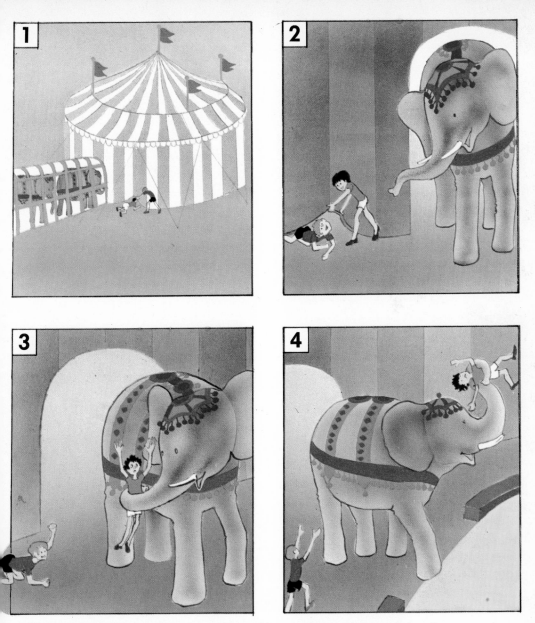

Tell the story from the pictures.   What are the boys doing?
Look at the second picture.   Where are the boys now?   What is
the elephant doing with the boy in green?   When you get to the
fourth picture, stop and think what might happen next.

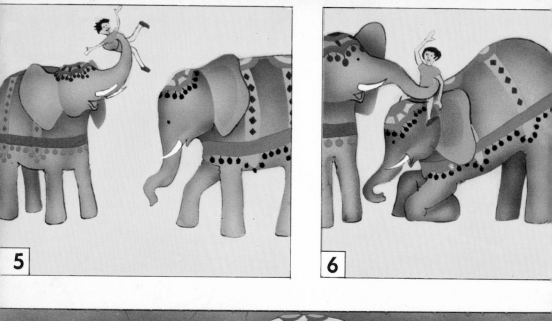

Look where the elephant is putting the boy.   Is the boy
pleased?   Would you like to ride on an elephant like this?
What do you think might happen now?

Look for the people on trapezes.   Look for the man on a
bicycle.   What is the man with the pole doing?   Can you see
people climbing a ladder?   How many people are on the
tightrope?   Which people are under and over it?

What animals can you see in this picture? Look at the different
families. How many children are there in each? Which family
is looking at the elephants? Why are the animals in cages?

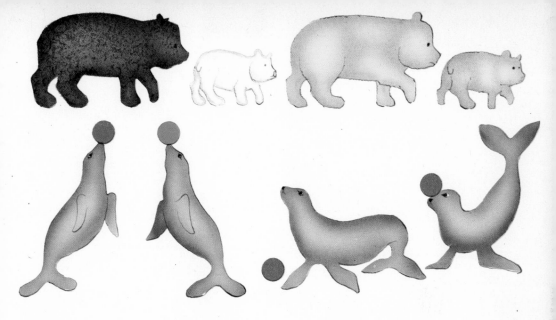

Count the bears and the tigers. Are there the same number of each? Count the seals. Do all the seals have balls on their noses? How many monkeys are there? What are they doing? Can you see an animal sleeping?

There are all kinds of things wrong in this picture. See how
many mistakes you can find.

What other mistakes could have been made?

For parents and teachers

These two pages give an indication of the theoretical background to each page of pictures. They are intended for anyone interested, but are not essential for using this book. We hope that the book will have succeeded if only it amuses, entertains and interests you and your child. Never make him feel that he has failed if he does not manage to answer the questions or understand the problems, and be generous with your praise when he does. He will, incidentally, be mastering skills which will help him to learn more easily later on.

The early years of life are increasingly being recognised as crucial in the intellectual development of a child. Skills of language and perception acquired in the pre-school years are the essential foundation for learning at school, and above all, for learning to read. Children with poor spoken vocabulary, and those who have difficulty in, for instance, noticing differences between shapes, colours and sounds, may be at a disadvantage when learning to read. The pictures in this book can be used to get your child talking, using new words, thinking, searching for and recognising details of shape, colour and meaning. It is important for you and your child to explore and discuss the pictures together. This will give him a chance to share his experience with you and learn about the adult way of looking at things.

Pages 1, 2, 3 & 4 These four pages should provide plenty to talk about with your child. Developing his spoken language by discussing pictures like these will enlarge the range of concepts he can use, and prepare him for the wider vocabulary he will meet when learning to read.

Young children do not naturally notice visual differences which may seem obvious to an adult. Many of the pictures we have devised should encourage your child to look more carefully and in differing ways.

Try to make your child think really hard about the possible outcomes of all the things happening on pages 1 & 2. He should learn that pictures, like printed words, can tell stories and give clues which enable him to 'predict' what may be coming next. Experienced readers probably 'predict' in very much the same way what the next word in a sentence is likely to be, and it is important that children should realise at an early stage that they will have to think about what they see in books, whether pictures or words.

Try to persuade your child to use his imagination to think out different consequences. Avoid giving him the impression that there is always a 'right' answer.
Page 5 In addition to a simple counting exercise, this page gives an opportunity to practice spotting differences such as the colours of the clothes and the harnesses, and the two clowns who are upside down.
Page 6 New approaches to teaching mathematics lay great emphasis on understanding that the same things can belong to different 'sets' at the same time. In this picture, for instance, the leopard lying down belongs to the set of leopards,